Fill in ☐   Copy ☐

c   h   d

_up   _ap

c   d   h   m

_og   _en

2

© Carol Doncaster and Joyce Sweeney 1995.
These pages may not be photocopied.

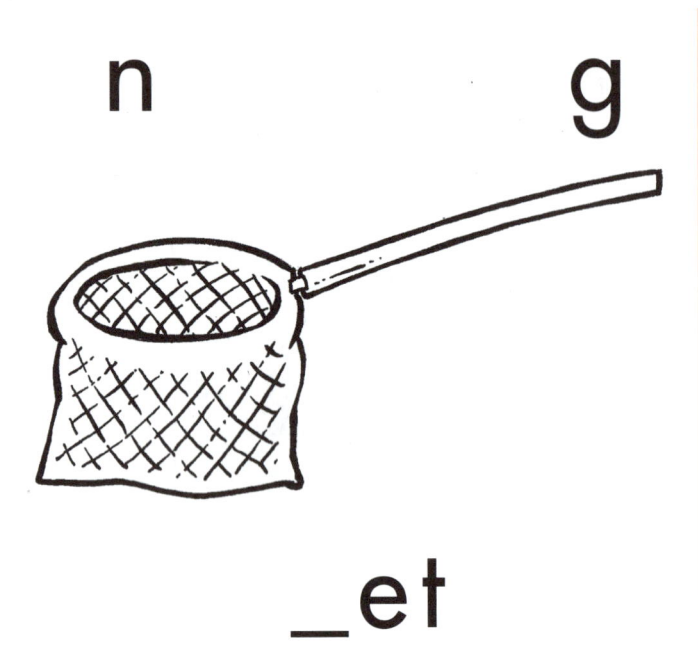

Fill in ☐   Copy ☐   Colour ☐

n   g   p   w

_et   _ot

....

f   w   f   p

_eb   _an

....

© Carol Doncaster and Joyce Sweeney 1995.
These pages may not be photocopied.

3

Fill in ☐   Copy ☐   Colour ☐

r   b   k   l

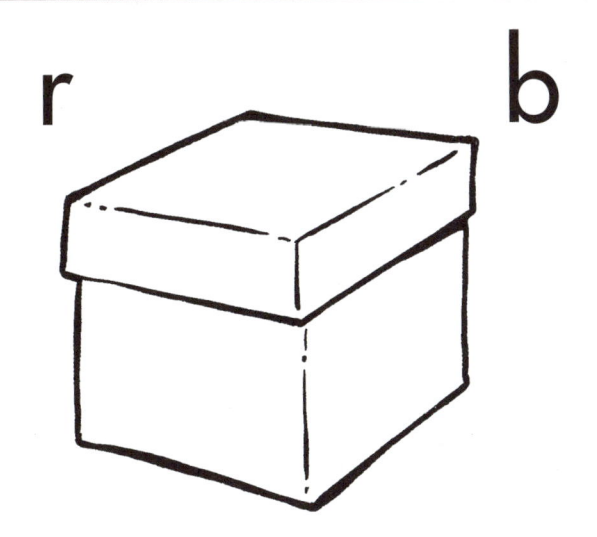

_ox   _id

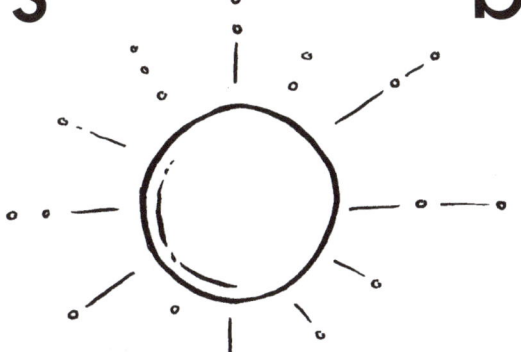

....

s   b   l   r

_un   _od

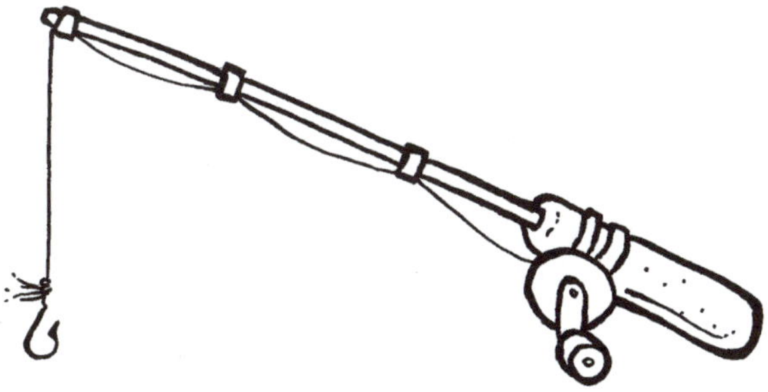

....

4

© Carol Doncaster and Joyce Sweeney 1995.
These pages may not be photocopied.

Fill in ☐   Copy ☐   Colour ☐

y   z   t   c

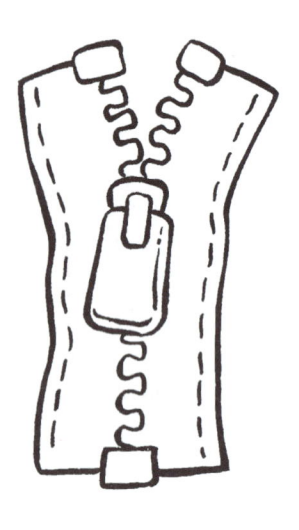

_ip   _ap

....

j   r   z   v

_ug   _an

....

© Carol Doncaster and Joyce Sweeney 1995.   5
These pages may not be photocopied.

Fill in ☐   Copy ☐   Colour ☐

b f j m r v

_ud

_en

_un

_ox

_et

_ug

6

© Carol Doncaster and Joyce Sweeney 1995.
These pages may not be photocopied.

Fill in ☐   Copy ☐   Colour ☐

s   h   l   p   c   w

_up

_ix

_in

_ig

_at

_og

© Carol Doncaster and Joyce Sweeney 1995.
These pages may not be photocopied.

7

Fill in ☐   Copy ☐   Colour ☐

d   k   n   t   z   s

_oll

_ig   _ag

_iss

_in

_ut

_un

8

© Carol Doncaster and Joyce Sweeney 1995.
These pages may not be photocopied.

Write ☐   Colour ☐

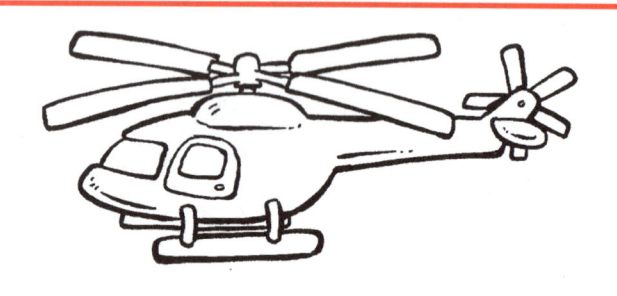

9

© Carol Doncaster and Joyce Sweeney 1995.
These pages may not be photocpied.

Write ☐ Colour ☐

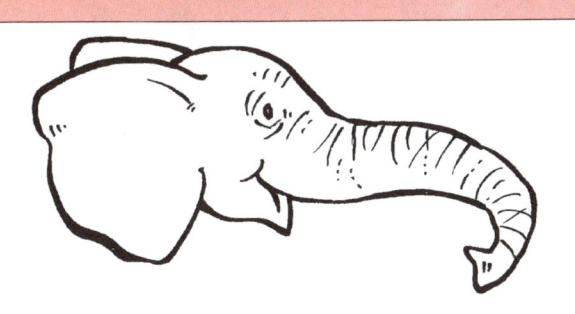

. . . .

. . . .

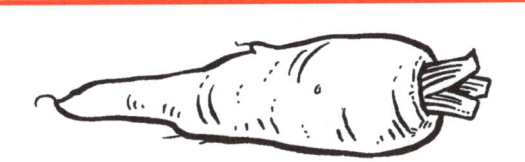

. . . .

. . . .

10

© Carol Doncaster and Joyce Sweeney 1995.
These pages may not be photocopied.

Write ☐   Colour ☐

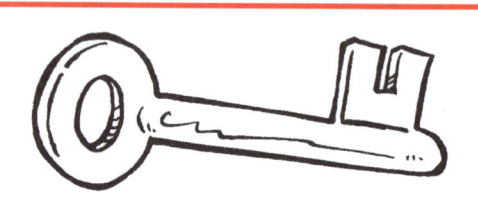

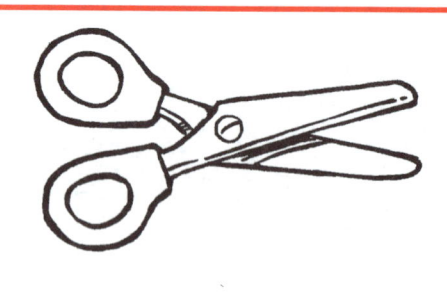

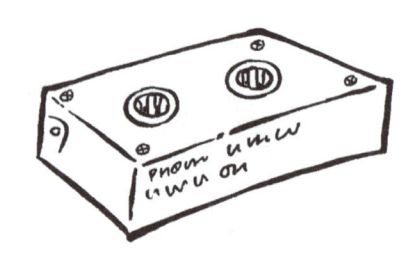

. . . .

. . . .

. . . .

. . . .

© Carol Doncaster and Joyce Sweeney 1995.
These pages may not be photocopied.

11

Write ☐   Colour ☐

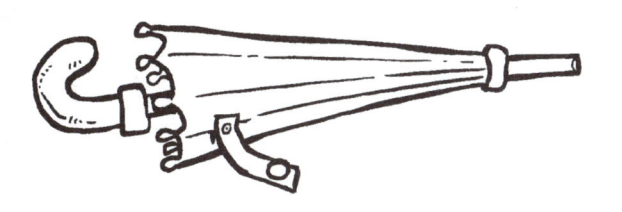

. . . .

. . . .

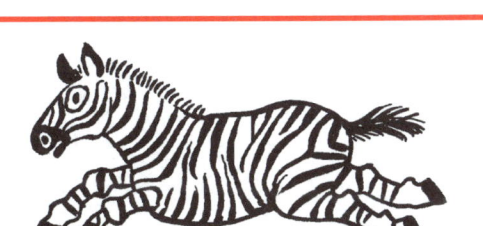

. . . .

. . . .

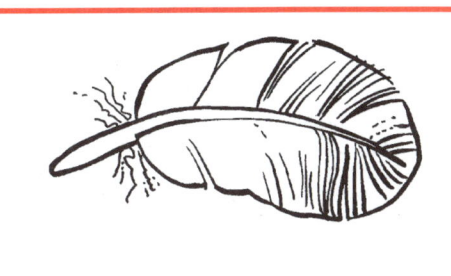

© Carol Doncaster and Joyce Sweeney 1995.
These pages may not be photocopied.

Match ☐   Colour ☐

ba

ja

ha

ma

ta

ra

la

sa

13

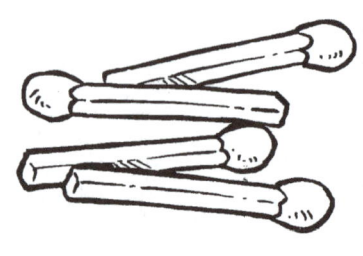

© Carol Doncaster and Joyce Sweeney 1995.
These pages may not be photocopied.

Match ☐   Colour ☐

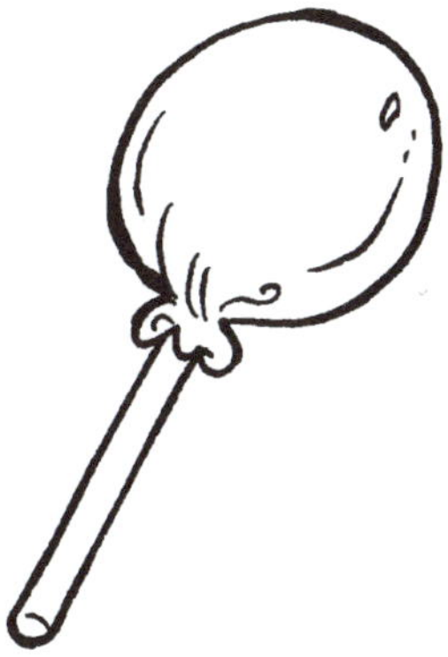

bo	ho
lo	mo
so	po
co	go

14

© Carol Doncaster and Joyce Sweeney 1995.
These pages may not be photocopied.

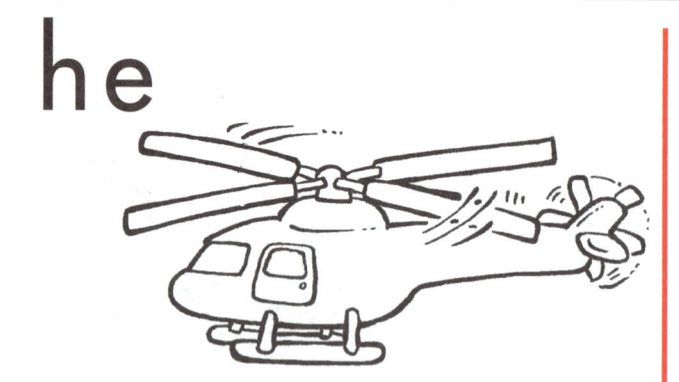

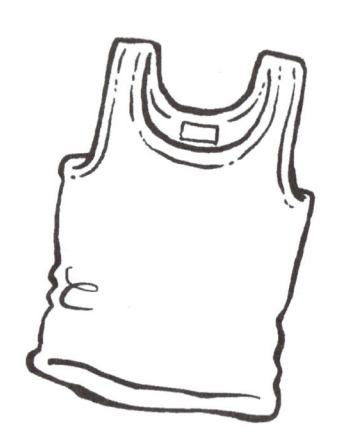

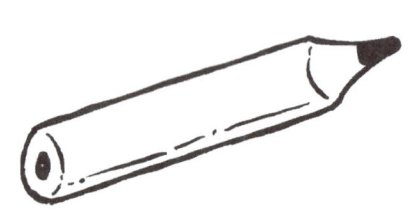

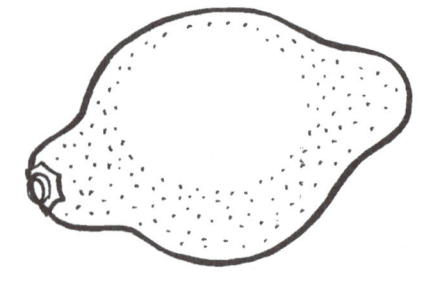

Match ☐   Colour ☐

he	ne
be	le
ve	me
pe	he

15

Match ☐   Colour ☐

bu

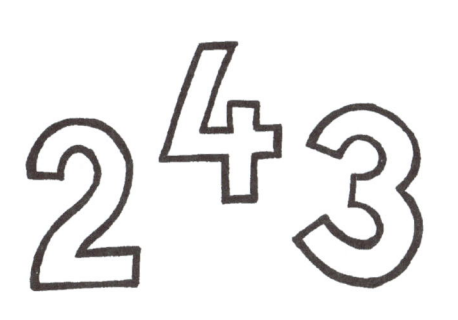

hu

su

du

ju

mu

nu

bu

16

© Carol Doncaster and Joyce Sweeney 1995.
These pages may not be photocopied.

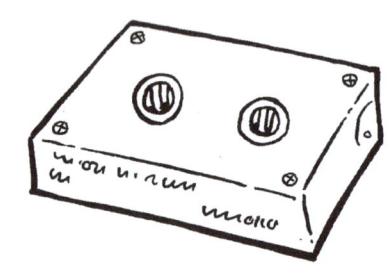

Match ☐   Colour ☐

wi		zi	
vi		ki	
ji		fi	
pi		hi	

© Carol Doncaster and Joyce Sweeney 1995.
These pages may not be photocopied.

Fill in ☐   Copy ☐   Colour ☐

ca   pa   ma   da

_ _n 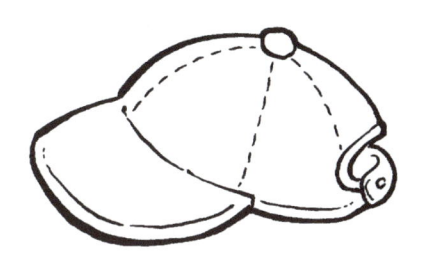   _ _p

....

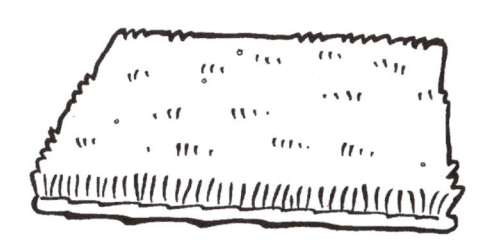

_ _t    _ _d

....

18

© Carol Doncaster and Joyce Sweeney 1995.
These pages may not be photocopied.

Fill in ☐   Copy ☐   Colour ☐

fo   co   ho   jo

_ _p   _ _g

....

_ _t   _ _x

....

19

Fill in ☐   Copy ☐   Colour ☐

be   we   pe   le

_ _ll

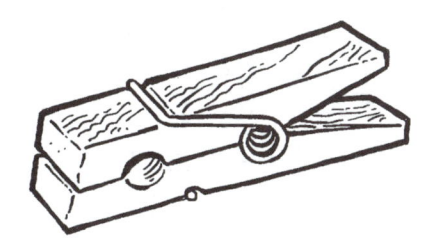

_ _g

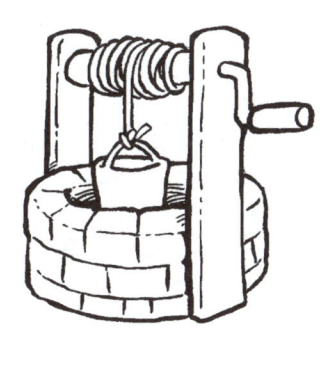

_ _ll

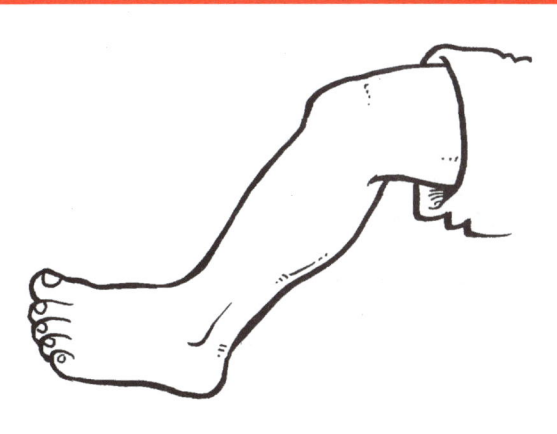

_ _g

20

© Carol Doncaster and Joyce Sweeney 1995.
These pages may not be photocopied.

Fill in ☐   Copy ☐   Colour ☐

ru   tu   hu   bu

_ _s   _ _t

_ _g   _ _b

21

Fill in ☐   Copy ☐   Colour ☐

mi   di   bi   si

_ _b    _ _tt

_ _x    _ _g

22
© Carol Doncaster and Joyce Sweeney 1995.
These pages may not be photocopied.

Read ☐   Find ☐   Write ☐   Colour ☐

_at	_an	_ag	_ap
cat	pan	rag	lap

© Carol Doncaster and Joyce Sweeney 1995.
These pages may not be photocopied.

Read ☐   Find ☐   Write ☐   Colour ☐

_ot	_od	_og	_op
got	pod	jog	pop

24

© Carol Doncaster and Joyce Sweeney 1995.
These pages may not be photocopied.

Read ☐   Find ☐   Write ☐   Colour ☐

_un	_ug	_ut	_ub
nun	hug	but	cub

25

Read ☐   Find ☐   Write ☐   Colour ☐

_et	_en	_ed	_eg
wet	men	fed	beg

26

© Carol Doncaster and Joyce Sweeney 1995.
These pages may not be photocopied.

Read ☐   Find ☐   Write ☐   Colour ☐

_in	_ip	_ix	_ig
fin	hip	fix	fig

© Carol Doncaster and Joyce Sweeney 1995.
These pages may not be photocopied.

Write ☐   Colour ☐

_ap

_un

_op

28

© Carol Doncaster and Joyce Sweeney 1995.
These pages may not be photocopied.

Write ☐   Colour ☐

_ut

_ox

_eg

© Carol Doncaster and Joyce Sweeney 1995.
These pages may not be photocopied.

29

Write ☐   Colour ☐

_an

_in   _at

30
© Carol Doncaster and Joyce Sweeney 1995.
These pages may not be photocopied.

Workbook A	000 312300-6
Workbook B	000 312301-4
Workbook 1	000 312302-2
Workbook 2	000 312303-0
Workbook 3	000 312304-9
Workbook 4	000 312305-7
Workbook 5	000 312306-5
Workbook 6	000 312307-3
Workbook Mixed Pack (1 of each)	000 312309-X
Teacher's Guide	000 312308-1

New Key Phonics is a carefully structured scheme of work to support children in developing phonic skills. It relates to both the National Curriculum and the Scottish 5–14.

Published by CollinsEducational
An imprint of HarperCollins*Publishers* Ltd
77-85 Fulham Palace Road
London W6 8JB

Cover designed by Neil Adams
Designed by Liz Black
Illustrated by Juliet Breese
Printed by Martins the Printers

© Carol Doncaster and Joyce Sweeney 1995

First published 1995

20 19 18 17 16 15 14 13

ISBN-13 978-0-00-312304-3
ISBN-10 0-00-312304-9

Carol Doncaster and Joyce Sweeney assert the moral right to be identified as the authors of this work.

All rights reserved. No part of this publication may be reproduced, stored in a retrieval system, or transmitted in any form or by any means, electronic, mechanical, photocopying, recording or otherwise, without either the prior permission of the Publisher or a licence permitting restricted copying in the United Kingdom issued by the Copyright Licensing Agency Ltd, 90 Tottenham Court Road, London W1P 9HE.

British Library Cataloguing in Publication Data

A catalogue record for this book is available from the British Library.

ISBN 0-00-312304-9

NEW Key Phonics

WORKBOOK 3

Carol Doncaster
Joyce Sweeney

Name

Collins Educational

Fill in ☐   Copy ☐   Colour ☐

c d

_at

....

h m

_ug

....

© Carol Doncaster and Joyce Sweeney 1995.
These pages may not be photocopied.

1